Summary
of

Killers of the Flower Moon
David Grann

Conversation Starters

By BookHabits

Tips for Using BookHabits Conversation Starters:

EVERY GOOD BOOK CONTAINS A WORLD FAR DEEPER THAN the surface of its pages. The characters and their world come alive through the words on the pages, yet the characters and its world still live on. Questions herein are designed to bring us beneath the surface of the page and invite us into the world that lives on. These questions can be used to:

- Foster a deeper understanding of the book
- Promote an atmosphere of discussion for groups
- Assist in the study of the book, either individually or corporately
- Explore unseen realms of the book as never seen before

About Us:

THROUGH YEARS OF EXPERIENCE AND FIELD EXPERTISE, from newspaper featured book clubs to local library chapters, *BookHabits* can bring your book discussion to life. Host your book party as we discuss some of today's most widely read books.

Table of Contents

Introducing *Killers of the Flower Moon*

*K*ILLERS OF THE FLOWER MOON IS A NONFICTION BOOK about how the Osage Native Americans were forced to leave their Kansas land in the 1870s, after being force onto the land around thirty years earlier. The Osage tribe was forced to a reservation in Oklahoma where the terrain was rocky, and the climate was dry. There were no more buffalo, and the land could not produce vegetation. The Osage tribe members started to starve. Then, oil was found in Gray Horse, Oklahoma, which was part of the Osage reservation.

After the oil was found, the Osage tribe received large amounts of money from prospectors looking to capitalize on their discovery. Every member of the Osage tribe suddenly found themselves being paid large amounts of money for the oil. They were able to build grand houses, buy cars, and hire servants. They became some of the richest people alive.

The large amount of wealth the Osage tribe acquired also made them a target for violence from white people. In the 1920s, for five years, over twenty Osage tribe members were murdered in some way. Some were shot, others were poisoned, and others found themselves the victims of car crashes. The people who murdered them were after their wealth and the oil that allowed them to become so wealthy.

As soon as the Osage tribe found oil, they were given white guardians. This is because the government of the United States did not believe that the Osage people would be able to manage their own finances. This was not a nice gesture. Instead, it was the government seeing the Osage people as unintelligent. The white guardians had to authorize every payment the Osage made. They had to authorize payments for even the smallest items, such as a tube of toothpaste. The white guardians were not at all trustworthy. They often stole money from the Osage. The merchants in Gray Horse, Oklahoma were not trustworthy either. They raised prices for the Osage.

When the Osage began turning up murdered in unique ways in large amounts, the tribe called it the "Siege of Terror." One woman who was affected by the Siege of Terror was Mollie Burkhart. Mollie was married to a white man named Ernest Burkhart. Mollie's sister Minnie suddenly died of an illness that was called a "wasting disease" back then. No one understood what the illness was. Next, her sister Anna was killed by being shot in the head.

Her sister Rita's house exploded one night at three in the morning. Mollie looked outside when she heard the explosion and saw a great fire where her sister's house once was. Rita, her husband, and their servant were all killed by the bomb which had been placed under the house. Finally, Mollie became gravely sick. She decided to barricade herself inside her home because she knew that she would be the next person to die. She realized that people were plotting to kill her family. She went out searching for justice for her family, and ended up putting a target on her back.

Attempts were made to solve the murders, but something mysterious would end up happening. Witnesses, lawyers, and friends of the Osage were murdered, and evidence would randomly disappear. At this point, the Director of the Federal Bureau of Investigation at the time, J. Edgar Hoover, became interested in the murders. Though, his motives were not entirely pure. He was trying to find a way to reinforce the strength of the Federal Bureau of Investigation at the time. The FBI was not allowed to make arrests, but they could investigate murders and other crimes.

Tom White, a man who was previously a Texas Ranger, was dispatched to Oklahoma by J. Edgar Hoover. White found that the murders were even more complicated than originally thought. Grann calls says it was like walking through a "wilderness of mirrors." Through investigation, White discovered that there was one person was the ringleader in organizing the murders. His name was Bill Hale, and he was a rancher in Osage County. His nephew was Ernest Burkhart. He convinced his nephew to marry an Osage woman, Mollie. Hale arranged the murders of Mollie's family in order to gain the rights to the oil. Hale, his two nephews, and a ranch hand named John Ramsey were all charged with the murders. However, the trial ended in a hung jury. Ernest Burkhart pled guilty. His wife, Mollie, had to sit in the courtroom and hear about how the man she had two children with killed her family. Later, more details came out about the murders when Ramsey confessed. This led to the conviction of both Ramsey and Hale.

Discussion Questions

"Get Ready to Enter a New World"

Tip: Begin with questions dealing with broader issues to ensure ample time for quality discussions. Read through all discussion questions before engaging.

~~~

question 1

Killers of the Flower Moon is about Native Americans who were forced from their lands and onto a reservation. What did you know of this topic before reading? What did you learn from reading *Killers of the Flower Moon*?

~~~

~~~

question 2

The subject of *Killers of the Flower Moon* is the Osage Native American tribe. How did your perception of Native Americans change after reading?

~~~

~~~

question 3

Killers of the Flower Moon details how the Osage Native Americans became wealthy after striking oil, which made them targets for murder. What do you think the author's motivation was for writing *Killers of the Flower Moon*?

~~~

~~~

question 4

The book is titled *Killers of the Flower Moon*. What do you think this title means?

~~~

~~~

question 5

Recently, Standing Rock has made news headlines with Native Americans protesting their land being used for a pipeline. What similarities are there between *Killers of the Flower Moon* and these current events?

~~~

~~~

question 6

In *Killers of the Flower Moon*, Grann writes that an Osage tribe member said that the question was not if the jury would consider this case a murder. It was whether they would consider a white man killing a Native American man murder. What did they mean by this?

~~~

~~~

question 7

The white people living in the area where the Osage lived seemed to be concerned about how the Osage spent their money, or even that they had money at all. Why do you think this was the general attitude towards the Osage?

~~~

~~~

question 8

In *Killers of the Flower Moon*, David Grann writes that "history is a merciless judge." What does he mean by this?

~~~

~~~

question 9

J. Edgar Hoover was concerned with strengthening the FBI during the time of the murders. Why was this so important to him?

~~~

~~~

question 10

Tom White was tasked with finding who was behind the Osage murders. What was your reaction when you found out the identities of the murderers?

~~~

~~~

question 11

The Osage tribe was treated unfairly by the United States government. What was your reaction to the treatment of the Osage?

~~~

~~~

question 12

Killers of the Flower Moon is a nonfiction book. How close to the truth do you think David Grann stayed when writing this book?

~~~

~~~

question 13

The United States government forced the Osage off their land twice. Why do you think they did this?

~~~

~~~

question 14

White guardians were assigned the the Osage people to "help" them manage their money. Why do you think they were assigned to this job?

~~~

~~~

question 15

J. Edgar Hoover played a role in trying to solve the Osage murders. Do you think he wanted to solve the murders to help the Osage, or was he acting out of his own self-interest and saw the murders as an opportunity?

~~~

~~~

question 16

The *Star Tribune* called *Killers of the Flower Moon* "fascinating." What was the most interesting part of the book for you?

~~~

~~~

question 17

Some readers found parts of *Killers of the Flower Moon* to be difficult to read. What sections were difficult for you to read?

~~~

~~~

question 18

A few readers are confused as to why the story of the Osage people is not
more well-known. Why do you think this is?

~~~

~~~

question 19

"Easy to read" was the way one reader described *Killers of the Flower Moon.*
What was your reading experience?

~~~

~~~

question 20

One reader described *Killers of the Flower Moon* as the best nonfiction book
they read in 2017. Others highly recommend the story. Why do you think this
book has become so popular?

~~~

Introducing the Author

D AVID GRANN WAS BORN ON MARCH 10, 1967 IN NEW YORK, New York. He attended Connecticut College where he studied Government. He earned his Bachelor of Arts degree from Connecticut College in 1989. He was a recipient of the Thomas J. Watson Fellowship. He went to Mexico to do research and began a career in journalism there. He attended The Fletcher School of Law and Diplomacy at Tufts University, where he studied International Relations and earned a Master's Degree in the subject.

In 1994, a year after earning his Master's Degree, Grann began working at *The Hill* as a copy editor. *The Hill* is located in Washington, D.C., and it covers United States Congress. At this time, he was also studying at Boston University. He earned a Master's Degree in Creative Writing from Boston University. He also taught Fiction and Creative Writing at the school. In 1995, he became the executive editor at *The Hill*. The following year, he was named the senior editor at *The New Republic*. In 2003, he became a staff writer at *The New Yorker*.

In 2005, David Grann was a nominee for the Michael Kelly Award. He was the recipient of the Sigma Delta Chi Award and the George Polk Award in 2009 for a piece he wrote for *The New Yorker*, entitled "Trial By Fire."

In 2009, David Grann published his first book, *The Lost City of Z*. *The Lost City of Z* is about Captain Percy Fawcett who disappeared in the Amazon in 1925 while looking for The Lost City of Z. People have been looking for the bodies of him, his son, and his party, as well as The Lost City of Z, for many decades. David Grann went to the Amazon to research the book and found that The Lost City of Z may have existed. He also found out how Captain Fawcett may have died. The film adaptation for The Lost City of Z was released in 2017 by Plan B and Paramount Pictures.

In 2010, David Grann's third book, *The Devil and Sherlock Holmes*, was published. The book is a collection of his essays published in *The New York Times Magazine, The Atlantic, The New Yorker,* and *The New Republic.* His most recent book, *Killers of the Flower Moon*, about the Osage Native American murders was published in 2017.

Fireside Questions

"What would you do?"

Tip: These questions can be a fun exercise as it spurs creativity among the readers by allowing alternate scene endings and "if this was you" questions.

~~~

question 21

David Grann does extensive research for his book, even going as far as the Amazon and meeting with Osage tribe members. What are your thoughts on this? Why do you think he conducts research this way?

~~~

~~~

question 22

Two of David Grann's books have been set in the 1920s. Why do you think he enjoys writing about this era?

~~~

~~~

question 23

David Grann only writes nonfiction stories. Why do you think he has never
branched out into other genres?

~~~

~~~

question 24

The Lost City of Z has been adapted for film. After reading *Killers of the Flower Moon*, would you be interested in a film adaptation of it?

~~~

~~~

question 25

David Grann has studied Government and International Relations. In what
ways has his education influenced his writing?

~~~

~~~

question 26

The events in *Killers of the Flower Moon* took place in the early 1900s. How would the events be different if they took place today?

~~~

~~~

question 27

Tom White and his men solved the mystery of the Osage murders. If you were given the task of trying to figure out who the murderer was, what would be your plan?

~~~

~~~

question 28

The Osage people suffered greatly when over twenty of them were murdered for their money. How do you think the tribe would look today if the murders had not happened?

~~~

~~~

question 29

Tom White was able to solve the mystery of the Osage murder. What would have happened if he did not?

~~~

~~~

question 30

Imagine you were living in Oklahoma during the Osage murders. What do you think your reaction to the murders would be?

~~~

Top 10 Amazing Facts

~~~

Top Fact #10

The land that the Osage lived on in Oklahoma was not a typical reservation. It was land that they bought themselves instead of land that was given to them by the government. When they bought the land, they managed to add in a provision that they would have ownership of all minerals on their land.

~~~

~~~

Top Fact #9

According to David Grann's research, the easiest way to kill the Osage was by poisoning them. This was because the police did not quite understand toxicology for poison.

~~~

~~~

Top Fact #8

When the Osage murders began happening, there was some local coverage on the murders. However, it did not gain much attention because the people being murdered were Native Americans.

~~~

~~~

Top Fact #7

In the 1920s, a lot of the justice being served to people was private. People often hired private investigators to help them with crimes, but the private investigators were often criminals themselves. Mollie hired private investigators, but they were often bribed to commit crimes while on the hunt for the murderer.

~~~

~~~

Top Fact #6

One man, Barney McBride was friends with the Osage. He tried to go to Washington, D.C. to get the federal government to help the Osage. However, he was kidnapped from his boarding house, then found naked, beaten, and stabbed later.

~~~

~~~

Top Fact #5

W. V. Vaughn was another man who went to investigate the Osage murders. He had a strong lead and called the sheriff to tell him of the information. Then, he disappeared. When his body was found, he was, again, stripped naked and thrown from a train.

~~~

~~~

Top Fact #4

When J. Edgar Hoover was starting the FBI, he was looking for agents that looked a certain way and had a college education. However, the agents lacked real experience in investigating crimes.

~~~

~~~

Top Fact #3

The FBI in the 1920s often released outlaws from jail that were supposed to work for them as informants. However, these informants often took their freedom and committed more crimes.

~~~

~~~

Top Fact #2

One of the problems facing the investigation was that the people who were being tried were able to buy people to be witnesses and jurors and to have witnesses killed. Quickly, the case went from wondering who did the crime to wondering if the suspects would be convicted of their crimes.

~~~

~~~

Top Fact #1

When doing research of the Osage tribe, David Grann was able to meet with Mary Jo Webb who is an elder in the Osage tribe. She was able to present Grann with records of her grandfather who had been killed during the Osage murders. She did her own investigating, like many other families, and found that there was many more people involved in crimes against the Osage than originally thought.

~~~

Quiz Questions

"Ready to Announce the Winners?"

Tip: Create a leaderboard and track scores to see who gets the most correct answers. Winners required. Prizes optional.

~~~

quiz question 1

Killers of the Flower Moon is a _____ book about the Osage tribe. The Osage were forced off their land and relocated to Oklahoma in the late 1800s.

~~~

~~~

quiz question 2

The land the Osage moved to was barren, and the members began to survive. Then, _____ was found on their land, and they became wealthy.

~~~

~~~

quiz question 3

Because they were so wealthy, they became a target for violence from white people. For a period of five years, the Osage tribe members were _____.

~~~

~~~

quiz question 4

True or False: The Osage tribe were considered to be incapable of managing their money on their own. For this reason, they were given white guardians.

~~~

~~~

quiz question 5

True or False: The Osage tribe considered the period of time where they were murdered to be a "Era of Murder." The members terrified to be in their homes.

~~~

~~~

quiz question 6

True or False: Mollie Burkhart was killed by gunshot. Her husband Ernest Burkhart was responsible for her death.

~~~

~~~

quiz question 7

True or False: People who attempted to solve the murders often wound up dead. Tom White was the man who finally solved who was responsible for the murders.

~~~

~~~

quiz question 8

David Grann was born in New York, New York in 1967. He studied
_____ at Connecticut College.

~~~

~~~

quiz question 9

David Grann studied _____ at The Fletcher
School of Law and Diplomacy. He later studied Creative Writing at Boston
University.

~~~

~~~

quiz question 10

David Grann went to _____ to do research. While he was there, he
began a career in journalism.

~~~

~~~

quiz question 11

True or False: The first book David Grann published was *The Lost City of Z* in 2009. *The Lost City of Z* is about the disappearance of a man in the 1920s who was looking for The Lost City of Z.

~~~

~~~

quiz question 12

True or False: The second book that David Grann published was *Killers of the Flower Moon*. The book is about the Osage murders in the 1920s.

~~~

Quiz Answers

1.   Nonfiction
2.   Oil
3.   Murdered
4.   True
5.   False
6.   False
7.   True
8.   Government
9.   International Relations
10. Mexico
11. True
12. False

Ways to Continue Your Reading

EVERY month, our team runs through a wide selection of books to pick the best titles for readers and reading groups, and promotes these titles to our thousands of readers – sometimes with free downloads, sale dates, and additional brochures.

Want to register yourself or a book group? It's free and takes 1-click.

Register here.

On the Next Page…

Please write us your reviews! Any length would be fine but we'd appreciate hearing you more! We'd be SO grateful.

Till next time,

BookHabits

"Loving Books is Actually a Habit"

Made in United States
North Haven, CT
04 August 2022

22238747R00039